Madonna Magdalene

Madonna Magdalene

Poems by ~~Kim Garcia~~

Kim Garcia

Turning Point

For Craig,
I'll be remembering
those opening
pages across
N.C.
Joy to your
Thanks,
KG

Charlotte, 2007

Published by Turning Point
P.O. Box 541106
Cincinnati, OH 45254-1106

Typeset in Galliard by WordTech Communications LLC, Cincinnati,
OH

ISBN: 1933456434
LCCN: 2006908360

Poetry Editor: Kevin Walzer
Business Editor: Lori Jareo

Visit us on the web at www.turningpointbooks.com

Acknowledgments

My thanks to the editors of the following publications in which these poems first appeared:

Harvard Divinity Bulletin: "Genesis Suite: Adam's Complaint, Eve's Answer, Cain"

Lullwater Review: "Bathsheba"

Mississippi Review: "Ash Milk Coal," "Mary," "Slaughter of the Innocents"

National Poetry Competition (Chester H. Jones Foundation): "Genesis Suite: Cain"

Negative Capability: "Mary Magdalene" (Eve of St. Agnes Contest)

Nimrod: "A Pause Between Larger Subjects," "Happiness," Rembrandt's *Danae*"

Open Windows: "Bestiary of Desire: Wren," "Cezanne's Still Life as Portrait of the Virgin," "Passion Sown," "Venetian Cloth"

Perpetuum Mobile: "Deep South Sleep," "The Land Was Made of Maps"

Redivider: "Bitten"

I would also like to thank the Oregon Arts Commission for an Individual Artist's Grant, the University of Houston for their Cambor Fellowship, and the Hambidge Center for the Arts for my much appreciated residencies.

My special thanks to my friends who helped me with these poems and encouraged me to complete them, especially Robert Alter, John Anderson, Valerie Anthony, Pam Ball, Emilie Boon, Van and Geoff Brock, Rachel Kadish, Pat MacEnulty, Sue Roberts, Terry Ruch, Liza Rutherford, Paul Shepherd, Lisa Steinman and Helen Wallace; faculty and friends (often one category) at Florida State

University and the University of Houston; and with special warmth, my husband Frank and my children Michael and Sarah.

Contents

For my teachers

For when the virgin's mind was illuminated
in God's mystic mysteries,
then wonderfully, a bright flower came out of her.
—Hildegard of Bingen

Madonna Magdalene

Place here the virgin in her Easter petals,
the ladder of green leaves, the open throat.
I was reading; my lamp was full. A bird
entered the room, and knocked the walls
with bright wings, drunk on sky-mindedness.

Here the story of my shame, pictured
above its tight band of explanation
no one reads. Here the stink
of animal dung on straw. Here milk,
and thorn to suck, the splintering nail.

Water to wine, we were stained
and intoxicated. Do as Love tells you.
Praise virginity lost, slow and conscious
as a strip tease. Layer by layer,
let it be done unto us. Again and again.

Part One: *King's Consort*

You blush like the dawn,
and like the sun's flame
you burn.
      —Hildegard of Bingen

Bathsheba

It is in the power of beginnings to shape all else.
So I stand before you in my husband's courtyard;
you lean upon your high wall and watch.
Cool water falls to the basin at my feet.

We wanted and we wed, but it was a dead man
who gave me away, cool hand in mine.
Seeing all, angry at little,
faithful past death.

In these last years, I have thought of him
in secret as my heart's companion.
Uriah, I'll say to the silence,
as I rock your child, *Uriah, it's hard.*

And he sympathizes, gentle and grave.
Like a well-paid servant, always present.
We speak of you, always you.
It was a love we held in common.

His beard brushed smooth,
his eyes calm and strangely gray.
He is guarding your door, your wife, your child.
Faithful Uriah.

Once in my husband's bed, I held my tongue
so as not to speak your name.
Now his hand is the breeze between our bodies.
His the invisible shoulder

that carries our child to burial.
In a palace cloistered in gossip,
I must hide what was once most apparent:

No, I am not your wife.

Santiago de Compostela

On the bridge a stone angel raises a sword
into a sky almost white with heat.
The stone of the bridge yells out
stone! heat! A wet stink
comes up from the river
sucked by the sky's intolerable thirst.
The candles at the base of the angel
have run together in one pool of wax
that smokes and answers thirst with thirst.

A dog with dirty yellow fur
runs the hot stones without interest
in the angel or the sky or the smoke.
Its begging tongue half out of its mouth.
Every step a simple prayer for water.

The old woman begging in the bar
turns the men from their *tapas*
with her silence. They give.
One hand out, white hair pulled back
in a bun smaller than a baby's fist,
she murmurs something so quietly and endlessly
that she could only be talking to God.

The farmers are burning what is left of their fields
now that the mustard flowers are gone.
It is the smoke's fleshy billows you see, not fire.
The smoke lit somewhere within.
In the slow train on the way to
Santiago de Compostela, the smell of the burning
fields comes in the open windows with the heat.

A young man with a rope for a belt
rests his feet on the box of young hawks
he has raised from stolen eggs.
He smiles, mouth half-empty of teeth,
a tan stomach where shirt buttons are missing.
I think of the stolen eggs
in a nest halfway between heaven and earth.
Think of his body hung from this rocky place,
and want it for where it's been.

Easter pilgrims walk the road to Compostela
on their knees, moving over stones
as smooth as eggs.
Each set by hand on a day no one remembers
but the laborer whose hand lovingly set it.
The penitents think of God,
or something like God, when they feel these stones.

I catch my shoe on one placed higher than another
and stumble for no other reason I can think of
than accident. It's the body
pilgrims take to Compostela,
hoping to settle the restless soul,
which I've passed through customs
again, undeclared.

Rembrandt's Danae

She doesn't look surprised, one jeweled wrist raised,
a second hand resting on the pillow,
patting it perhaps. "Come on over here."
The way one talks to money. A forthright,
boarding house intimacy that comforts
even the immortals who lie down one
dark gold disk at a time, scale from their thoughts
a too-vast omnipotence, and get real.
The old woman catching back the curtain
is not surprised either. She's the future.
She's counting out the present's coin, knowing
that the night's shower fronts the morning's drought.
Over the bed Cupid wrings manacled
hands—no more tricks. Here blindness is banished.

Judas

i.

In the end I am almost motionless,
braiding in loops and tangles, a line,
copper-bright, between you and me.

When the world unhinged its jaws
and brought its lips together
in a withered pucker, I noticed.

Perhaps God took the old life,
the thread of the old life,
and wound it into a ball for a better soul.

Maybe good intentions can be sold
and resold
like a birthright.

ii.

Love has the acceleration of a falling body.
I thought you loved as I loved,
a single essence, a specific weight. I was sure.
I loved the things of earth that were in you.
Your words were grain, your body bread and wine.
Marketplace stuff, handled by shopkeepers.
I knew your price to the last denarius.

iii.

There are rocks within
of unknown substance.
Things that congeal and cool,

upon which hope can break.
So we love, unequally, and stumble, upon death, equally.

iv.

To tell the story of a kiss
the whole story of it, from beginning to end,
I must have time.

A kiss must slip between the pages of intention,
a moment of thoughtlessness,
within a desert of design.

Without such grace it is only the lips' mark,
a position of the organs,
no more to be remarked upon

than a rock on the ground,
or this rope joined to my hand:
the world's hard currency.

v.

They would not take the silver
they paid for my kiss,
not even for the grave I am seeking.

It is blood money, they said.
God will not touch it.

The second sweet-smelling flower of my flesh
begins its blooming. The second life
which is the body's decay.

It is a rose. Take it,
my love's last offering.

vi.

I cannot stop these colors from running
together, forming black.
I cannot stop myself from rushing
in fear through this last, slow kiss.

The pupil slowly shrinks
under the sun's radiance,
like the circle of a noose,
like the hungry plush of a kiss.

Desdemona

There is no purity without its blemish
and I loved with a darkness your skin sang.

You tasted of battle and blood, and I loved
your murderer's heart heedlessly. I sinned,

back when you questioned no cloth—you looked.
You had ears and eyes, and hands that shook

when you scored my heart, pulsing wet. I sinned
when I kissed that knife. Husband, I'm sinning yet.

Black Water, Texas Belles

            Tides, the double-
edged brush of a wet tongue
up and down the river,
every grain of sand dreaming pearl.

            We are waiting
for periods, lunch, boy scouts
from the camp upriver
under the Texas pines.
The water is warm.

            We squat
in the mud in shorts, and squeeze
the brown silt through clenched
palms, listening
to the Doobie Brothers singing

            Black Water
over the sateen of the slow river's
body with its moccasin snarls,
copperheads among the roots,
and imagine gators, second lids

            peeled for prey.
They are like us, slow
to open their mouths
mute and dangerous, wrapped
one day as handbags
and shoes, made useful,

and having laid hold
of something, unable to let go.
We are drugged with sun,
with the knowledge that we
will never be more valuable
than we are right now—
lying there in our skins.

Fra Angelico's Mary Magdalene and the Risen Christ

He is rising; the trees and grass have the false precision
of botanical prints. And neither the hoe he carries in his hand,
nor the look she extends like a lead bar, is grave
enough to moor the helium of his resurrection.

Her arms are heavier than her torso can bear. She is mortal,
draped in cloth with the physical properties of rock,
burdened with the counterweight to his ascension.
They can meet only on this page.

Even here his feet float over the carefully untouched grass.
His palm hovers like a saucer on the air.
They are fixed in this moonscape, moment extending,
through the impossible physics of longing,

which runs precisely equal and opposite.
They have eyes only for each other. This we understand.

Little Women

Is this Pilgrim's Progress, Alcott's theater of peace?
Fevered scenes scarcely less stilted than a dress
rehearsal of Jo's own creation. Who plays the father?
The empty boots are in the attic, where a single light
burns, a flame for that angel who may never marry
and winter witness to the dying men, some who may

march to that Eternal City on the Hill, which may
be all a Boston soldier knows of paradise or peace.
Jo's best silk is singed at the back. But she must marry.
She stands gripping a single, soiled glove. The dress
with its burnt gash is turned away from the candlelight
in the ballroom where the Brahmins whisper of her father

serving at Shiloh or Antietam, where four score of fathers
and the sons of Boston too poor for substitutes may
die (like the local Irish) of wartime shortages or freeze in light
uniforms, no shoes, nothing in their bellies but the Union's dried peas.
A sheet of snow turns them to draped silhouettes, bloody feet dressed
in white, no longer thinking of the little women they'll never marry.

Beth's hands and feet are hot, then cold. In her infirmary
some dolls have no arms or legs. The babies have no fathers.
All winter, fires burn the sweat-drenched suits and dresses,
fruits of a fever which infects the poor of Boston and may
have begun in the dark of the battlefields' unnatural peace
where Barton's lamp wanders wherever the dying call, "Light!"

The knapsack falls from the pilgrim's shoulders, light
as it was. Beth is dead. She will never marry.
Her hand in Jo's is a crumpled glove. Peace
wears its gash, the color of dried blood, torn farther

than Grant's north, Lee's south. Jo wants to die. She may
die. She is losing her hair, the war, the will to redress

the gash of this poverty—Emerson's upright riches dressed
in wounds, opening like the glaring slats of pure light
Thoreau reported between the wall boards at Walden in May,
when winter was still far off, and Boston's infirmary
was not filled with those too poor for self-reliance; fathers'
limbs frittered away like so much detail, heavy, in pieces.

Little Woman, put on this wedding dress. You will marry.
The glorious are scorched to ash and light, fallen into their fathers.
Battle as you may, you will wed this crippled peace.

The Bishop Undresses

first the collar then

the breath,   then

long hands

       emptied of their host

body and blood   drop

then   coat

black shirt black legs

shield and skin   then

flayed   then

the body's scapular

       horsehair, knotted with blood. Then

looking in the glass

then

Where hast thou lain him?

Genesis Suite: *Adam's Complaint*

In the morning as I put on clothes by the fire
I hear you pouring milk from bucket to pitcher
singing snatches of a song I don't know.
Secrets on your face.

You've veiled yourself from me, Eve.
The taste in my mouth is sharp and bitter,
dead dust caught up by the plow
and blown into my face.

I have not forgotten your perfection.
Before you, I slept.
I sit on the step as the sun goes down.
My hands are gold in the last sunlight,
and then go dark.

The house glows white in the dusk,
and the tree above cracks and knocks its fingers
together in a light wind.
I think of you in the darkening house,
how we never speak together.

Page from the Apocalypse, Illuminated

The virgin escapes, book in hand,
while the dragon with its seven heads,
each preaching she's a whore,
spits smoke and water into its own black hole.
The land is parched, the trees carry
broken limbs like thoughts forgotten, still felt.
She rises horizontal, stiff in gold.
Her eyes rest on the spine of the closed book,
Tales of Babylon, lifted from the heart's shelf.
She carries it tenderly, almost hungrily,
as they are drawn across the sky as one.

Anniversary

We promised
something very much like this, an estimate
or rough sketch. Who could imagine how big
the rooms would feel? The sizes of childhood!
Instead of three steps—six—to cross the room,
and even then we haven't reached the door
which is years and years from here.

I am
constantly measuring things out, trying
to take these bearings. Are we married yet?
Can I get that in real numbers? *We promised*
something very much like this, this rough sketch.

This field,
temporary track at best, laid out on grass,
where all hands race their horses and bet
wages on a chalkboard ghosted again
with last week's losses. *Who could imagine how big*
these would feel? The sizes of childhood!

We are
imprecise in our longings, calling love a field,
its sum a door, dogged in miscalculation, insisting,
instead of three steps—six—to cross the room.

But look
how every year we arrive at the same present,
newly chalked, a love recalculated and run
to a horizon that leaps its vanishing point,
and even then we haven't reached the door

which is years and years from here,
an eternity like childhood.

Mary Magdalene

When the wood splintered and broke,
we answered as you answer in grief,
poorly, with whatever comes to hand.
And took down
what we could scarce tell from stone.
What had been breath and blood
and substance.
Now heavy as clay,
building block of those things
that sit low and heavy on the earth.
We might have stretched him
between house and house,
and written on the post of his thin hip
a trespasser's warning.
Or we might have laid him
among the stones of the Roman road.
And their chariots, our slow carts,
might have passed over him.
And the driver,
looking down at the reins in his hands,
then up at the horizon,
notice nothing but his own thoughts.

This was his death:
the wrapping of the sheet about the ankle,
the sound of wet woman's breathing at the head,
the body, heavy with harsh refusal,
leaving us to carry all.

It came to me as wild animals
first retreat from the light of the fire,
and then creep back.

Ringing the light with eyes
and the sound of their breath.
Until the soul of the animal swallows
the light of the fire
and it is only a small ember
in the great expanse of the belly,
which is the glad, animal night.
And the stars themselves circle the isolated earth
with one ravenous, joyous intention,
and are looked on in turn
by the solemn, secretive ring of angels.
So, in the center of all things came my knowing.
When Osirius pressed a gem of honey
and amber into my navel and lay upon it,
didn't I know happiness? Or when
the dark-faced one left a halo of gold coins
on my pillow, and I stretched in a glad, empty bed,
while the morning air smelled of tired donkeys
and laborers—they so poor, me so suddenly wealthy—
didn't happiness come and take me by the shoulders
and shake me until my earrings rang like bells?

And in the dark,
lit by the hot smell of lamp oil and sweat,
when I looked over the hill of shoulder,
shaking as it was with its own storm,
wrapped in its own misery and passion,
like a woman in childbirth,
didn't I find pleasure in my cool,
well-watered kingdom?
A fish who swims too deep for the net.
Placid, like the paving stone
of a walled and shaded garden.

I did not repent the flesh.
Flesh finds flesh as brick finds brick.

Our mothers clasped us round at our birthings,
and our fathers caressed us into arms and legs.
I repented that my heart lay still among my ribs
and did not once
flap and break itself against the bone.
I repented that in the pressing of flesh
I found no agony.

This was the Lord's last gift
to Mary Magdalene:
an agony,
a parable in flesh,
a plundering of past pleasure.

Part Two: Desire's Bright Flower

Now let it please you
to burn in that love.
—Hlidegaard of Bingen

In the Narita Airport, 1997

Your flight was delayed. Mine was early.
Karma blooming on coincidence.
I remember your sixteen year old body
entwined with mine on the living room rug
as we twisted ourselves into a character
that suggested something between
will and won't—a form we thought
uniquely ours, and therefore indelible.

Like the ancient Japanese cherry trees,
propped on bamboo in the postures
of their first spring,
we carry each other in rings of forgetting
then remembering again.
This trunk, these limbs.

Time is the clothing we negotiate now
as we stand in this public place
saying things we might say to strangers.
Every leafless word an axe
to that beauty which never bore.

Genesis Suite: Eve's Answer

                        We were
like stones falling, too stupid
with obedience to grieve. God waited
on my thoughts: my tongue

drenched with possibility.
The world began
to work at last, to turn over, to die
and stink of change, and birth up fresh dying,
to rot, to labor and begin again.

                        I knew
the name. I saw what might be or have been. Each
moment tied to the next in flesh, all breath kin.
No beast told me this because no creature knew it.

Only God's fingers, that joyful grasping inside me,
could have seized such sight.
Only God within you
could have been tempted by it.

                        What evil can come
of such a joyful beginning?

Bestiary of Desire: Dog

Each pad a blood-swollen grape.
Nails drag the pavement. Exhaustion
like sand between the sheets of muscle
that twitch. Every hair an itching nettle.

The bones are the only thing that doesn't hurt.
A meatless cage that carries the heart.
No movement free of desire's choreography.
Tongue, a single gutter leaking thirst.

Lucky dog, you will plunge nose-first into the bucket,
you will drink up the water in silent barks.
You will walk three times around your rest
and find it, stretched on cold tile, playing dead.

As a snake

unhinges its jaw
and the skin bursts
on the fallen fruit
so that wasps
can come and eat their fill,
the hollow beneath my words
tears into this grammar,
this prim book of years
with its ruthless bliss.

Easement

I grew up under wires
that hummed just below
hearing, and caught
our kites, rasping
sheets of plastic
every spring.

Big Texas storms
came in off the Gulf—
sky segmented by towers
bright as blades
against unnatural dark.
Why tell you this?
The green and the black
before the storm
are still hanging
somewhere in Texas.

I am still awkward
and full of water.
The morning glories have closed
their throats,
tight blue joints
finger the thunder.
The crawdads are half out
half in their mud daub huts,
waiting for the lightning
that brings the rain
so they can fish again
clay pools alive with current.

Bestiary of Desire: Heron

Pines, grown for paper, stiff as pencils.
The oaks at water's edge, curled against the salt.
Between groves, a single restless crow.

Long-legged heron, a graceful articulation
in water brackish as a kiss, tasting of more thirst.
The silent snap of its twigged legs, kindling.

It wraps the air before it in an embrace
of great wings that lifts its feet.
The air tastes of snails. Your skin is fresh water.

Bitten

So long that the dog roses have dried and gone, St. Augustine crept
        over the wild grass,
fences knocked down, boards rotted with termites, pulled down,
        cicadas crushed,
nothing left but this love and a rattler's head, lying in the run-off,
        teeming with fire ants,
fangs still holding venom, its promise of wild sleep, even as its eyes
        are eaten away.

The Little Golden books my mother saved in the garage have dampened,
        darkened
 page by page, even the bright girls in raingear, the ducks—everyone
        eyes open.
Wasps outside the kitchen door have given up the nest my father sprayed
with his poison. The bird skeleton I found in the attic insulation is dust.

Go on. You walked across that field and into my yard, you knocked
        the wasp nest
out of the eaves, you buried the bird and took my father's poison.
        What more
could he do? Each wet page of my book dried and curled, even
        as a rain swamped
the hard blades of St. Augustine, every one a warning never minded,
        never missed.

Walk me out, fence by fence. Dog roses are climbing
        my drugged limbs
where each thorn burns. Fire ant, rattler, termite—hurry
        this house down.

Bestiary of Desire: Squirrels

The squirrels are outside the upstairs windows,
running the same paths they ran this same time
last year. The same supple limb dips and climbs
with their weight, resumes its dignified shadow.
Flea'd snarls of hair-fine nerve, ecstasy's fools,
who forgive and forget what they bury;
I'm shamed by the pure carelessness of squirrels,
hungry but light-footed in the leafless tree,
while I palm once more an old finished thing,
which I swear I put into the ground myself,
promising you it was gone, and buried well,
but come back to me now—moldy, smelling
of dirt and the rain that's fallen, me not
remembering since last time I dug it out.

Southern Aubade

The sun spills its lacquer
over the late summer leaves
on tired stems. The woods'
green milk is ladled into the day.

Here I am, as I've always been,
half-listening. The striped fly
without its usual buzz
lands. I'm waiting. I have a hand

in the world as we perceive it.
The dead branch is barked in fragile moss—
a length of pale gray smoke
which rests, barely breathing.

You can't love like this, I tell myself:
nameless, wordless. Beneath each leaf
some loveliness passes unremarked.

Bestiary of Desire: Crow

I won't fly with dark sails to feast again.
The storm freezes fast the blooming ground
and under the fallen trees dogs are chained.
Hungry, beaten to silence, cowed.

And yet the jays and squirrels hound me still.
Their young grown feathered and furred, hauled
away by the world's lust for more bloom, willing
more death; where I come in like one called. Called.

Eager

Above the snow, a single maple holding forth
its dying flame. Among the feats of Nature:
                                                    the wild
greening from dry bulb, sour alchemy of rot, a rusty
        handprint of lichen;
                                                    the eager
space-seeking species springing up after fire,
as though they took no lesson from destruction
but to begin again, twice as joyful.

They call all experience of the senses mystic, when
the experience is considered
                                            —D. H. *Lawrence*

All the great lovers are brown, like thrushes
or wrens, with their eager uplifted tails
their small, hidden nests, eggs warmed
in shit and straw, settled in the hollow
their own breasts have made, with singing.

                            Give me a stone
when I ask for bread. Give me a snake
when I say fish. Give me the senses
when I say God, and God when I call
for light—*first light, last light. Light.*

This is a catbird's song. Sounds like thrush, like
wren. Like a lover, not so great, not so God, small brown
mystic, a hidden stone snaking, my eager fish.
All sense uplifted. Shit uplifted. Straw uplifted.

Why call for light? There's plenty of light.
Why call for God? There's plenty of God.

Morning

The early planets' glow
is eclipsed by the growing light.
We are clumsy seducers
of the day's mysteries,
watching only the sun's rise.
Out, out the small candles,
night's sparks, moon's mirror.

I don't speak here for Melancholy
but for light's own truth, dimmed
as happiness is, diversion-sprung.
Play is refraction seen, reflecting
this day's gentle indirection.

Bestiary of Desire: Wolf

Lovely are the little, red girls
and the littlest has become round.
So—bang—we're coming. The fanged
are beloved of the sun. Golden.

Under the trees we roll in dirt.
River glances of liquid silver. The girls
become wives. Our pups are wild.
They nuzzle with teeth of pearl.

Beloved also of the moon,
silver-tipped like the pines.
Passion's cold vibrato,
senses roving in packs.

Easter Vigil

The bishop, the only black man in this Southern church,
carries the golden shepherd's crook, lights
the candle that lights another, and on,
until the church is filled with yellow, wavering light,
cheap wax threatening to gutter out, the hot smell
of material in resistance to becoming flame.
                          Grease of miracles,
beads of melt, snake to the cardboard holders.
The door gusts shut against the night's bonfire.
We're left this broken alleluia with bells,
this stumbling along to benediction,
willing ourselves to be finished,
                          and never finished.
The year's great candle is dipped in the fount.
Wax cools on the marble-cold waters.
The lector raises her arms.
Babies, come to be baptized, cry against the hour,
against their stiff Easter swaddling, against the incense
that scorches the waxy scent of small children's hands
carefully coloring the Lamb and lilies.
                          The language of arrival
presses down, nearly burying joy in its assurances
while the body on the cross
strains up, as any dancer can see,
burning this spring night's dark myrrh.

Venetian Cloth

Against warp, the weave is a silken pulse
with that illusion of intimacy
small, repeated acts manufacture.
Bound by contradiction, threads stubbornly
gesture towards their separate horizons.
Conflicts resume the old patterns again.
Why call a thing lovely that only lasts?
Here our silver-blue happiness is twinned
to heartache. But here, my love, we begin afresh.

Bestiary of Desire: Wren

Cicadas whistle like teakettles and then suddenly drop
off, while three shrill jays hound a silent crow from his pine.

The afternoon's green is poached with heat, yolk-broken
under a black lid of clouds. Drops heavy as small frogs land warm

on the leaves, paper hands clapping, falling thicker and
faster until the air is a rush of tinsel, determined to cleanse the
earth at last.

Thunder rolls logs, snaps kindling in a halogen blink of
sight, which reveals a startled world, caught in the act of bowing,

until at last the storm relents, its dream of ruthless
utopia wrung out. Water stands in depressions like clothes
dropped in an affair

that ended badly. Nobody wants to reclaim them. Bit by bit
the ground tactfully mops up.

Then the wren starts, testing the sodden wing of its voice
as its tail keeps time, marking its quick breath's urgency.

The sun arrives suddenly and the day's brightest green is
thrown out to it, a last effort to harvest light into sugar in the hour
before dusk.

Passion Sown

Behold, the sower went out to sow...
—Matt. 13:3,4

Beside the road
the birds of the air are happy,
quick-hopping in this shower
of unearned, unsung plenty,
scouring the stones with beaks
sharp as needles. Wasting nothing.
Each seed ground to a meal
in their rocky gullets.
They will rise from the road
whistling for more.
The same tune as last year
and the year before.
Knowing there will be more
thrown in lovers' haste.

Upon the rocky places
passion springs up
driving every promise
into a newborn want—
a single blade
pointing the way
all hopes fly.
And having said all
there is to say,
passion burns
the last sugar
from its eager tongue
and is carried away
on the wind's open palms.

Among thorns
the dull and fearful leach
every saving from the soil.
They hoard sunlight
in thorns and tight husks,
lack seed thought
or bee-summoning bloom.
A too-generous love
says *"What can we do*
but lean down to them
and love them?
Let them weave their thirst
into our overflowing green?"
It believes it cannot be spent.

Everything the sun said to us
we found we could answer.
It was all there—in the good ground,
which yielded to the fragile,
the root-tipped, to what finds a way
by seeking it blindly, by touch.
Rain dripped down into dark
and rose, fleshed in fruit:
hip, berry, and bloom. Again
we shout for the sower,
for life with legs,
to come now and take us
where none of our kind has been.

A Pause Between Larger Subjects

Creation, say desert thinkers, is an absence.
The sky naked of stars, a palpable silence,
the void—a virginity so pregnant
that it quickly yields to confinement.

No absence without containment,
no innocence without experience.
The quicksilver skin of a bubble
concealing the sphere of exquisite vacancy.

It's the unformed word on the tongue
before wind and wet and the cultured
contours of mouth and teeth
spin and cut the vowels with consonants,

like the three old women of Norse legend
who sit at the roots of the Tree of the World
and measure out life and death in embroidery silks:
gold thread for the rich man, brown for the poor.

Scarlet for the one somewhere in the middle
who isn't hungry for the next word
or sated by the last, but pares the round new cheese
he holds in his lap, with a pocket knife.

He watches the pale crescents form under the knife
pauses and turns the bulk in his lap.
Comparing it in his mind to some impossibly perfect round,
and now and then, to the distant and barren moon.

Cezanne's Still Life as Portrait of the Virgin

The lily cloth is gathered in blue folds
as if it concealed something,
folded upon nothing but itself.

Spheres of orange and yellow in thick rinds,
softened out of perfection by what passes
for human clumsiness, burn steadily.

The busy knife is stopped. Cloud's light
stilled on the belly of the pitcher.
The oranges just touch.

From this place we might see Cezanne's mountain,
a glorious mistress. And from there,
with unframed sight, all we have ever loved.

Tree in the Shape of a Hebrew Letter

The bark flamed with late winter light.
We stood and looked and walked again.
I was afraid to take off so much as a glove,
burning up with the possibilities
simple flesh might hold,
burning but never consumed.

We followed a stream,
not directly but meandering
as the path took us,
half-hidden in leaves
and the dusk which fell in
close to the water.

That flaming bark,
a cage of roots
filled with damp leaves,
and your gloves on my hands
are all that is left
of that day's implosion of wanting.

There was nothing at the end of the path
so we walked out the way we came,
playing out what I remember
as a very thin conversation,
reversing the possibilities
we walked in with.

We passed the tree twice,
going in, coming out.
I touched it both times.
A thing I loved without understanding.

Part Three: Bearing

"You are a blossom
which the winter
of the serpent's breath
did not harm."
　　　　—Hildegard of Bingen

Ash, Milk, Coal

Ash
A breast pocket of crackling cigars,
a knee as big as my back.
My head is covered by a warm hand.
The fire pops like a rifle.

Hoofprints the shape of my own sex
are pressed into the cement of the hearth.
They are clear and clean of ash.
He has built this cabin with his hands.

Milk
The water lips the lakeshore.
I run a finger along your temple
where the hair meets skin.
A lover's nerve endings are thin and
vibrating as spider's silk stretched
invisibly over the water to catch
shivering, silvery minnows
which might or might not rise.

The belly of the frog is spilling with eggs,
a thousand jelly eyes pulsing.
A snapping turtle, furred in pond scum,
cleans among the cattails by moonlight.
The water is the color of milk.

My lips nuzzle your unshaven chin.
An unweaned creature sucking the jaw's hard bone
for nourishment too old and slippery
for the machinery of speech.

Coal

You are born perfect, little man, and screaming.
I am crumpled on the bed like your old, shed skin.
Your name means "like unto God"
and this is the way God loves:
He puts a hot coal on your tongue.
He cracks your hips like the spine of a book.
He breaks open the body and augurs the burst soul.

The Land Was Made of Maps

and the maps were perfect, of perfect places,
of those places we think of when we think of you, of me,

and wish we were somehow better or different
than we are—the kind of landscape we draw on cash:

Mt. Kilimanjaro, Mt. Fuji, a rolling plain; everything done
in fine inks, which can't be counterfeited, in spidery lines,

shock waves, Richter shivers of vibration like a mountain
registered on the skin of our desire to be beloved, muscular always;

until those points where maps meet are fused and become
a mountain, famously beloved. Where we are perfect.

Deep South Sleep

The day is sunk in a deep
state of gestation.
Cottoned into sleep
on the long bench of Florida
a lung of lime seeped
in the bathwater it half rose from.

The first day's down, time's dew hairs
are on this living thing.
shell bones crackling underfoot,
jasmine threading this moment's
labyrinth, dragging the sweet reek
of last winter's dead.

The land's green plush is veined
with slow brown rivers
reversing with distant tides.
A sinkhole's blue eye stares
into the scorched sky, soaking
each reflected wing in its socket.

I am drugged on so much lushness,
inclined to nap, the old potion
closing the bloom of sight,
like an over-stimulated infant.
Each leaf is a supple card
shuffling, shuffling,
in endless, whispering hands.

Genesis Suite: Cain

It is a fresh-fallen world,
and Cain is master of it.
First tooth, first step, first word.
He will be second in nothing.

The raw yoke of the sun
runs warm light over his downy back.
The stone floor is furred with gold.
Cain's day is fat and vigorous;
and what he sees, he possesses whole.

In the night his cradle rocks
under the open window
as he moves his heavy head,
round and white as the moon,
from side to side.

He dreams what all children will dream:
endless, indivisible dominion.
His small hands grip hard
against the rough cotton under his body.
Soft nails scratch quietly as they move.

The moonlight slides over his body
making the new down on his head
cold, bright silver
and all his body white with light.

Slaughter of the Innocents

for my son

My son is two days old and screaming.
The nurse puts new blood into my arm.
Blood goes in, milk goes out.
She introduces me to what's left of my body.

At twenty-five I have a city of desires
each an infant
crying ceaselessly after milk.
Like Herod,

I must suffocate one in its sleep,
put another to the sword. I cry,
childlike, and will not be comforted.
I am softened at every bone.
I am nothing but milk.

There is only one child
who will survive the slaughter,
only one wise and willing mother.
That woman can not be me,
but, Michael, let the child be you.

Mary

When he nurses at my breast
his breath is warm and sweet like incense.
I know the number of each curl,
and my arms encircle him like a halo.
For God Himself this should be enough.

The women of the village walk by our window.
The breeze in their cloaks saying "hush."
And their sandals patting softly on their heels
like a mother's hand on her sleeping child.
This moonless night is impregnated with stars.
The darkness overshadows us with gentle wings,
and we, if we are wise,
let it be done unto us.

On a warm night I lay this child
on the table by the lamp.
His fist in his mouth—this one fist,
this particular mouth.
I wash his feet, his legs, his belly.
I turn him on his side,
run the cool cloth up his warm back,
and he startles, eyes open.
I am saying, "This is a body.
Make your peace with it."

Now the olives are in flower,
but they will be plucked and pressed,
and pressed again
until the oil that is left is harsh and bitter.
My son, on that day
take me into Paradise.

*On the way back from Halifax we received word
that Carlos had died*/Roethke's carnations

diving into a pool, while his friends looked on, breaking his neck.
Pale blossoms, each balanced on a single jointed stem

My book was open to a poem by Roethke. The alders bowed.
And leaves curled back in elaborate Corinthian scrolls;

My own son was in Berlin, beginning to mourn for the first time,
the air cool, as if drifting down from wet hemlocks,

Would we ever get him back? We were drifting,
or rising out of ferns not far from water—

nothing could be decided. We looked at the sea, clear of fog,
a crisp hyacinthine coolness.

Then as we drove up to the cottage the whales came
like that clear autumnal weather of eternity

On another day we would have said, what good luck! Oh Carlos,
The windless perpetual morning above a September cloud.

Coaxing

When you were two
you loved nothing
from my hand.

I laid new toys
on the floor
and pretended to read.

I coaxed you to the breast,
to the bottle, in and out
of your jacket, into the world.

Taste and see.
Taste and see.

You chewed stick and sand,
as I hugged my knees
to my chest on the cement bench

and watched your hands
catch and release
every pleasure and plague

a public playground offers.
Palm out, I drew close to you
so you could spit into my hand.

A mash of red berry, leaf mould
and grit. It was bitter, but you
wailed when I dug it from your cheek.

How could we know? We were
very young. And every course
was laid out in front of us, beckoning.

Michael

Whose name is "like unto God" after the angel of violence.
Whose first word was the squall of a cat made mighty and manful.
Who would sleep when he must nurse, and cry when he must
      sleep.
Who was thin, red, and angry proclaiming a straw-born
      wretchedness.
Who delights in water equal with dirt.
Who glories in repetition, as God's own measure.
Who is Word, being both machine and spirit.
Who will probe even the phone jack, with his finger, unto
      its inmost workings.
Who will observe, thereupon, his mother's terror with the calm
      of eternity.
Who will persist in this dark and electric navel of the wall
      for wisdom's sake.
Who is spanked most heartily, and joins his mother in weeping.
Who will cling to the one who has hurt him.
Who will look to the jack with longing and bless it: *Death,*
      nameless Friend.
Who will embrace his death one day with an intimacy that
      eclipses all others.
Who comforts his mother of this knowledge.

If I Could Die

If I could die, and the things left behind forget me
and the ones left behind forget me
and the words I am speaking now forget me
and what remembers in me forget me
and what I call God forget me

then will I rest in peace
and peace will forget me;
and forgetting peace
I will, a thing,
forget my will
forget my words,
my peace. My God,
if I could.

Epiphany

We walk in paper crowns
around the darkened rooms
led by a dinner candle.
Sprinkling the last of the holy water,
singing the last Christmas songs.

The names of the three kings
are chalked over the lintel of the front door
under a sky sparsely lit with stars.
By faith, there is one for each child born tonight
but there is too much street light to see it.

Inside again, we sit in kitchen chairs
around Baby Jesus, crowned in beeswax,
standing in a velvet doll's chair.
The wise men are frozen in a three part tableau
of completion: walking, standing, kneeling.
Mary twists in her graceful s-curve of yielding.

My child lies long and heavy
with his head in the crook of my arm.
He traces the outline of my face,
remakes it with sweaty fingers,
smelling of dinner.

"*Pax*," I want to say to such love, "Uncle," "I give up."
You are the immovable object, you are the
       irresistible force.

The Child Goes Missing

He wasn't there, not where we'd agreed. I'd specified *that chair*.
He wasn't there. I asked a stranger to check the airport bathroom.
A stranger! He disappeared into that washroom of strangers where
a seven-year-old boy could go stranger and stranger, and come back
on the back of milk cartons and sad flyers tacked to school bulletin
boards and telephone poles. From the doorway I heard someone flush.
The stranger came out. He wasn't there.

                           Everywhere boys not him.
A hall full of gateways, thresholds to international airports of small,
dirty, fourth-worlds or fourth wards of deviants and maladjusteds
whose mothers probably lost them in airports *just like this*,
on days as simple as this was, suddenly snarled into a story
which just gets worse and worse, while nothing happens fast enough
except my fears which have lifted off, landing gear hanging,
cabin pressure dropping,

                         running the length of that hall
at the end of which I see
he and his father walking casually
among the sane.
I collapse. And then,
as they wave distantly
like tourists visiting my recent unpleasantness,

                      I am refueled with maternity gone mad,
and I can't decide whether I will kill my son and then his father,
or strike first that charming snake who sired the child who is
slithering sideways now behind his father
as we come within eyebounds, and I see flash across his lids
that chair.

                      I want to ground him for a month,
bind him to my hip, put a chip under his skin, which will transmit at all times
and all places: *Let no stone bruise your heel, no thorn crown your head.*

Didn't you know? he says, *I'd be with Dad?* I couldn't speak.
I knelt, I pressed my head against his chest. I wept.

Walking the Dog

The gibbous moon is caught in the pond's wet palm.
      Bullfrogs, those leggy bellows, wheeze out the summer

while we walk through a field of last year's Christmas trees,
      stumps cut flush with the ground. This black lab wants it all.

He wants to jump in the water and lap up the lop-
      sided moon. He wants to catch the frogs. He wants

to pull me through the fields of buttercups and grass
      to a wasp-covered road kill and broken-backed voles.

His path dead-ends in an overgrown hollow of flame
      azaleas and rhododendrons. We have to stop.

but the dog, chuffing at his chain and choke collar
      wants to go on, will always just want to go on.

He has the world in his nose, the dark wood blossoms
      with scent and flavor. He drools. And what heart would

pull him back from the bushes, just end here and now
      what he would only abandon out of exhaustion?

Stupid dog, I say. While he waits, eyes on the woods,
      for me to stop talking to myself and go on.

Happiness

The red berries I crushed last year
            are back on the bushes.

Fall's hard-shelled buds
            engorged with flesh and seed.

Even the leaves are caught
            with sugar on their hands.

I prayed to be older and wiser;
            This is what happened.

last night, whale cove

a pod of whales' deep-lunged blow passing the mouth of the cove
as the three children fall to sleep, girls talking long lines of insistence

and incredulous lift—the boy knocking on the wall, they answering
with taps to the floor, the creak of the beds—limbs brush and shush

in the sheets, across the walls, ring on the metal bedsteads, water
over rocks, pocking and trickling, and then yessing up the beach—

we lie in bed, two people gathering the middle to our beginning
feeling young in the world, hearing loon, whale, child, water.

Out of joy, I took on the most clownish and exaggerated
mode of expression possible
                    —*Rimbaud*

I walked into the room and lifted a book, not entirely guileless.
                              And the face I'd pressed
between the pages was still there, intent, eager in its season. And you

were there too, not quite yourself, but soft to the touch. I stroked
the velvety undersides of your wrists, wept into the plush of my own

feeling. When we felt need of a change in scenery, we pulled a bolt
of brocade slowly, hand over hand, along the wall. There was nothing

to it really, hardly a prop. A single door, hollow as a wasp's nest,
          never slammed
quite shut. Maybe a paper mache pan, a stack of newspapers,
          a jar of pencils

without erasers. One day we gave away the chair and sat in each other's
laps, watching the walls tell the same stories again and again, under

the floating ceiling, painted like the sun and the sea, in the sky together.

Kim Garcia's work has appeared in *The Harvard Divinity Bulletin*, *The Atlanta Review*, *Rosebud*, *Nimrod*, *Cimarron Review*, *Mississippi Review*, *Brightleaf*, *Scribner's Best of the Fiction Workshops*, *Negative Capability*, and *Lullwater Review,* among others. She is the recipient of an AWP Intro Writing Award, a Hambidge Fellowship and an Oregon Individual Artist Grant. A graduate of Reed College, she teaches creative writing at Boston College. She can be reached at www.kim-garcia.com.

Printed in the United States
71434LV00005B/67-81